Slow Cooker
Soup Cookbook

Easy Crock Pot
Soup Meal Recipes

Louise Davidson

— THE —

COOK🍳BOOK

PUBLISHER

Contents

Introduction

We all have special, heart-warming memories involving soup – eating alphabet soup as a child and spelling your name with the letters, your mom offering you chicken soup to make you feel better when you were down with the flu (and it really worked!), sitting on a cozy chair on a harsh cold night and sipping a hearty stew, being on a date while sipping a delightfully exotic and flavorful soup with a name you couldn't pronounce (that was the moment you thought "I've finally found the right one") — so many memories that warm us up inside and make us smile.

This cookbook wants you to relive all the wonderful memories you have about soup and make even more of them. Picture yourself coming home after a hectic, stressful day. Just as you open your door, the inviting and invigorating aroma of fresh hot soup wafts towards your nostrils…just as though Grandma had sneaked into your home to surprise you with her nourishing brew. Within minutes, dinner is served and the whole family can enjoy a satisfying meal together.

Yes, the slow cooker (also called a crock pot) can be your magic genie or the shoemaker's elves, doing the work for you while you sleep or while you have other things to do. You throw in all your ingredients, leave it and come back for a ready-to-eat meal. You save time, energy and money but still turn out healthy and delicious food.

Slow cookers are for the seasoned chef as well as the cooking novice because of their versatility. With the slow cooker, you have time to do other stuff. The slow cooker is also safe to leave cooking all day in your home. You can prepare soups to warm you in winter. In summer, while using the well-insulated pot, you can prepare tasty dishes without adding more heat to your home.

The recipes in this cookbook have been organized to make sure you get a great-tasting soup. They range from super simple to slightly elaborate. There are traditional soups as well as soups inspired by different cultures. It will be an exciting adventure.

So, turn the page and begin making new soup dishes that you and your family will remember forever!

The Goodness of Soups

Soup is known to be chock-full of nutrients because of the variety of possible ingredient combinations — you can combine meat, vegetables, grains, spices, herbs, and fruit. It can be a full meal, a side dish, a snack or, in some cultures, even a dessert. Not only is it easy to prepare and tasty, it can be economical as well. Soup can be filling and satisfying, making it ideal for weight management. In many cultures, soups are a panacea for all sorts of ailments.

Because of the combination of proteins, carbohydrates, and other nutrients, as well as the easy-digestibility of soup, it gives a steady supply of energy to our bodies. The boost of energy, the ample nourishment and the warm memories we associate with soup makes it the perfect comfort food.

Tips for Making Soups in the Slow Cooker

The slow cooker is a versatile appliance. It may even be used for roasting and baking. But it is with soups that the possibilities seem endless. Cooking in the slow cooker offers the convenience of dumping everything in and walking away and later coming back to a ready meal. There are some ways, however, to get more flavor and better quality from the ingredients. Here are some helpful pointers:

- The size and capacity of your cooker (from 3.5L to 6.5L) should match your needs and the quantity of food you have to prepare. The quantity of ingredients in the recipe should also match the capacity of the cooker. Overfilling and spillage will be detrimental to both the food and the slow cooker.
- Study the instruction manual carefully.
- Different brands and models heat up and perform differently, so you may have to make your own adjustments in cooking time. You'll have to experiment at the beginning. Follow the initial cooking times given. If the main ingredients are not done yet, continue cooking. Check every 30 minutes or so until you've determined the right cooking time for your slow cooker.
- Cut ingredients in similar sizes for even cooking.
- To get the best results, the slow cooker should be half to three-quarters full. **Liquid** should cover the contents by about ½ inch. Remember that there is hardly any evaporation while cooking in a slow

cooker, so not much liquid is needed compared to a regular stove-top cooking.

- Place longer-cooking ingredients like **meats** and **root vegetables** at the bottom where they will be in contact with direct heat.

- Use LOW heat as much as possible. A longer cooking time also means more time for flavors to develop and meld, giving a more delicious result. **Meat dishes** usually cook from 6-10 hours while **vegetarian dishes** cook from 4-6 hours.

- Inexpensive **meat cuts** which are tougher are ideal because the longer cooking time will make them moist, tender and fall-off-the bone. Some recipes call for searing or browning before adding to the slow cooker to enhance the flavor of your soup. There are slow cookers that have inserts that can be used for searing on the stove top and later placed back in the slow cooker, doing away with the need for a skillet or frying pan. Others do away with this procedure and still give good results.

- Do not be tempted to add more **wine** or **liquor** than called for in the recipe. **Alcohol** does not evaporate as much in the slow cooker as it would on the stove top. This would result in a raw alcohol taste.

- Add **rice, noodles,** and most **grains** near the end of the cooking time so that they don't get too mushy.

- **Beans** (except canned beans) are usually soaked 5-12 hours or overnight and drained to remove harmful toxins. Soaking also supposedly enhances the taste and texture of the beans. Many slow cooker recipes do not require pre-soaking. **Kidney beans,** however, definitely have to be soaked or rapid-boiled for 10 minutes and drained before putting in the slow cooker. Adding **salt** at the start of cooking is said to help keep the bean intact. Also, remember to remove any dirt or unhealthy-looking beans before using them in your recipe.

- Keep the lid on unless the recipe says otherwise. Lifting the lid even for a short while might require another 30 minutes of cooking time just to return to the right temperature.
- More **onions** and **garlic** may be added, compared to stove-top recipes, for better flavor release. Use larger cuts so that flavor release is in time with the cooking.
- Crush **peppercorns** and **seeds** (like **fennel** and **cumin**).
- **Herbs** like **rosemary** and **thyme** release better flavor when fresh. Stems and leaves may be added as well but be sure to remove them before serving.
- Fresh **spices** like **chilies** can be added at the end of cooking time, cooking just long enough to release flavor.
- **Milk**, **cream**, **cheese**, and other **dairy** should be added towards the end of cooking time to avoid curdling.
- **Fish** and **seafood** should be added towards the end as these cook quickly. Delicate fish will turn too flaky if cooked for too long.
- **Coconut milk** should be added towards the end to prevent the oil from separating.
- **Cornstarch** or **flour** for thickening should be whisked with a little water to make a slurry and added at the end.

Get to know your slow cooker well and try out the recipes. Once you've become familiar with how your slow cooker works, you'll achieve consistently wonderful results!

Caring for Your Slow Cooker

Your slow cooker's instruction manual contains the most pertinent information for caring for your slow cooker. Here are some basic tips:

- Try not to cook longer than the cooking time given in the recipe so the food doesn't get burned.
- Do not add cold ingredients to a slow cooker that has already been heated. The insert is sensitive and may crack or break.
- Turn off, unplug and allow your slow cooker to cool down before cleaning.
- The heating base should not be submerged in water or any liquid.
- Always remove the lid first before removing the insert or stoneware.
- The slow cooker insert is dishwasher safe. When using the dishwasher isn't enough, the following may be used:
  - hot, soapy water
  - baking soda (for gentle scrubbing)
  - vinegar
- Use a slow cooker liner or non-stick cooking spray for easy cleaning after cooking.

Remember these simple tips and you'll be able to use your slow cooker for many meals and through many happy family occasions!

Beef Recipes

Beef Soup with Barley

Serves: 8

Preparation time: 10 minutes

Cooking time: 8-9 hours on LOW or 4 hours on HIGH

Ingredients:

2 pounds boneless beef chuck steak, cut into 2-inch pieces

4 cloves garlic, minced

1 onion, chopped

2 pounds baby carrots

1 cup white mushrooms, sliced

2 stalks celery, chopped

1 cup pearl barley, uncooked

48 ounces beef broth, reduced sodium and fat free (6 cups)

1 8-ounce can tomato sauce

⅛ cup Worcestershire sauce

Salt and pepper

Fresh parsley, chopped, for garnish

Directions:

1. Put all the ingredients, except parsley, in the slow cooker. Stir.

2. Cook for 8-9 hours on LOW or for 4 hours on HIGH.

3. Serve garnished with chopped parsley

Nutrition (per serving)

Calories 275

Fat 6 g

Carbs 28 g

Protein 28 g

Sodium 290 mg

Irish Stew

Serves: 8

Preparation time: 15 minutes

Cooking time: 8 hours on LOW

Ingredients:

2 pounds stew beef, cubed

1 large onion, sliced

5 carrots, cut to about the same size as beef cubes

1 14 ½-ounce can tomatoes, diced

1 8-ounce can tomato sauce

¾ cup pearl barley, uncooked, rinsed and drained

5 cups beef broth

1 cup water

3 stalks celery, chopped

1 bay leaf

½ teaspoon sage

½ teaspoon thyme

Salt and pepper

Directions:

1. Place all the ingredients in the slow cooker, and stir.
2. Cover and cook 8 hours on LOW. The soup is done when the beef is tender.
3. Remove the bay leaf and serve.

Nutrition (per serving):

Calories 415

Fat 15 g

Carbs 36 g

Protein 27 g

Sodium 740 mg

Bacon Cheeseburger Soup

Serves: 6-8

Preparation time: 15 minutes

Cooking time: 7 hours on LOW

Ingredients:

1 pound ground beef

1 cup onion, chopped

4 cloves garlic, minced

2 tablespoons cooking oil

1 14 ½-ounce can tomatoes, diced

1/3 cup bacon bits

½ cup celery, chopped

1 cup carrots, shredded

2 cups potatoes, cubed

8 ounces cream cheese, cubed

4 cups chicken broth

1 teaspoon dried basil

1 teaspoon dried parsley

Salt and pepper

¼ cup flour

1 cup milk

2 cups shredded cheddar cheese

Directions:

1. Sauté the beef, onion, and garlic in a skillet over medium heat. Make sure the meat is browned evenly. Place in the slow cooker.
2. Add the tomatoes, bacon bits, celery, carrots, potatoes, cream cheese, chicken broth, basil, parsley, salt, and pepper, and mix.
3. Cover and cook for 6 hours 50 minutes on LOW.
4. Whisk the milk and flour together to make a slurry.
5. Add the slurry to the stew along with the shredded cheese.
6. Cook 10 minutes longer to thicken and until the cheese has melted.

Nutrition (per serving):

Calories 630

Fat 17 g

Carbs 85 g

Protein 38 g

Sodium 2,312 mg

Beef and Cabbage Soup

Serves: 10

Preparation time: 15 minutes

Cooking time: 8 hours on LOW

Ingredients:

1 pound beef stew meat, cut into ¾-inch pieces

2 tablespoons cooking oil

Salt and pepper

1 medium-sized green cabbage, shredded

6 tomatoes, crushed

1 large onion, finely chopped

6 cups beef stock, divided

3 cups water

2 cloves garlic, minced

¼ teaspoon dried basil

¼ teaspoon dried oregano

Sugar to taste

Directions:

1. Use a 6-quart slow cooker to accommodate the volume of shredded cabbage.
2. Pat the beef dry with towels and season with salt and pepper.
3. Add oil to a skillet and sear the meat over medium heat. Meat pieces must be evenly browned.

4. Add about 3 cups of beef stock to the skillet and bring to a bowl. Stir and scrape the brown bits. Pour into the slow cooker.
5. Place the cabbage, tomatoes, onion, remaining beef stock, water, garlic, basil, and oregano in the slow cooker.
6. Cook for 10 hours on LOW.
7. Add sugar according to taste.
8. The flavor of the soup is enhanced after refrigeration or freezing. May be kept in the refrigerator for up to 5 days.

Nutrition (per serving):

Calories 176

Fat 3 g

Carbs 15 g

Protein 13 g

Sodium 816 mg

Beef Tomato Macaroni Soup

Serves: 8-10

Preparation time: 15 minutes

Cooking time: 8-10 hours on LOW

Ingredients:

1 pound ground beef

1 large onion, diced

3 cloves garlic, minced

6 cups beef broth

1 28-ounce can chopped tomatoes

1 28-ounce can whole tomatoes

½ cup ketchup

1 ½ tablespoons Worcestershire sauce

Brown sugar to taste

1 teaspoon Italian seasoning

2 cups dry macaroni

Salt and pepper

Directions:

1. Season the beef with salt and pepper and brown, together with onion and garlic, over medium heat in a frying pan. The beef is ready when no longer pink.

2. Drain away the grease, and transfer the mixture to a slow cooker.

3. Add the beef broth, tomatoes, ketchup, Worcestershire sauce, brown sugar, and Italian seasoning.

4. Cover and cook for 8-10 hours on LOW. The beef should be tender.

5. Add the dry macaroni 20-25 minutes before the end of the cooking time. Serve when the macaroni is tender.

Nutrition (per serving):

Calories 261

Fat 17 g

Carbs 15 g

Protein 13 g

Sodium 727 mg

Hungryman Stew

Serves: 8

Preparation time: 20 minutes

Cooking time: 6-8 hours on LOW

Ingredients:

1 pound ground beef

1 medium onion, sliced

1 tablespoon cooking oil

2 cups carrots, diced

3 russet potatoes, diced

1 16-ounce can kidney beans, drained

¼ cup uncooked long grain rice

1 8-ounce can tomato sauce

4 cups water

¼ teaspoon chili powder

¼ cup Worcestershire sauce

Non-stick cooking spray

Directions:

1. Coat the slow cooker with non-stick cooking spray.
2. In a skillet, heat the oil and brown the meat and onion. Drain off the grease and transfer meat to slow cooker.

3. Add the carrots, potatoes, kidney beans, rice, tomato sauce, water, chili powder, and Worcestershire sauce.

4. Cover and cook 6-8 hours on LOW. If the potatoes and rice are still too firm after 6 hours of cooking, continue cooking for another hour, and then check every 30 minutes or so for doneness.

Nutrition (per serving):

Calories 274

Fat 12 g

Carbs 27 g

Protein 14 g

Sodium 342 mg

Healthy, Hearty Pot Roast Stew

Serves: 8

Preparation time: 15 minutes

Cooking time: 6-8 hours on LOW, 4- 5 hours on HIGH

Ingredients:

2 pounds boneless beef chuck pot roast, trimmed and cut into 1 ½-inch cubes

¼ cup all-purpose flour

1 teaspoon dried thyme

½ teaspoon ground black pepper

4 tablespoons olive oil

1 large onion, chopped

3 cloves garlic, minced

3 cups beef broth, low sodium

3 tablespoons tomato paste

1 28-ounce can diced tomatoes, undrained

½ teaspoon salt

16 ounces fresh baby Portabella mushrooms, diced

1 medium sweet red pepper, chopped

2 stalks of celery, chopped

1 cup carrots, chopped

Fresh Italian parsley

Directions:

1. Pat beef cubes dry with paper towels.
2. Combine the flour, thyme, and black pepper. Toss with the beef cubes to coat.
3. Put the olive oil in a skillet and sear the coated beef over medium heat. Brown evenly and transfer to a slow cooker.
4. Add the onion, garlic, beef broth, tomato paste, tomatoes, salt, mushrooms, red pepper, celery, and carrots.
5. Cover and cook for 6 to 8 hours on LOW or for 4 to 5 hours on HIGH.
6. Garnish with parsley and serve.

Nutrition (per serving):

Calories 265

Fat 11 g

Carbs 16 g

Protein 28 g

Sodium 743 mg

Traditional Vegetable Beef Soup

Serves: 8

Preparation time: 15 minutes

Cooking time: 8-10 hours on LOW, 4-5 hours on HIGH

Ingredients:

1 pound beef stew meat, cut into 1-inch cubes

1 24-ounce package frozen mixed vegetables, thawed

4 cup red potatoes, diced

1 large onion, diced

1 15-ounce can diced tomatoes, undrained

1 15-ounce can Great Northern beans, drained

1 32-ounce carton beef broth

Salt and pepper

1 teaspoon garlic, minced

2 bay leaves

1 tablespoon vegetable oil

Directions:

1. Pat the beef cubes dry with paper towels. Season with salt and pepper.
2. Put olive oil in a skillet and sear the coated beef over medium heat. Brown evenly and transfer to a slow cooker.

29

3. Add the frozen vegetables, potatoes, onion, tomato, beans, broth, salt, pepper, garlic, and bay leaves. Stir and cover.
4. Cook for 8-10 hours on LOW or for 4-5 hours on HIGH. The stew is ready when the beef and potatoes are tender.
5. Remove the bay leaves and serve.

Nutrition (per serving):

Calories 262

Fat 5 g

Carbs 25 g

Protein 28 g

Sodium 290 mg

Beef Bourguignon Chunky Soup

Serves: 10

Preparation time: 10 minutes

Cooking time: 6-8 hours on LOW

Ingredients:

2 tablespoons olive oil

2 pounds stewing beef, cut in 1 ½-inch pieces

1 teaspoon salt

1 teaspoon black pepper, freshly crushed

2 tablespoons flour

1 bundle fresh thyme

½ cup cognac

2 cups beef broth

2 cups Burgundy or any other dry red wine

1 ½ tablespoons tomato paste

4 cloves garlic, minced

1 large onion, sliced

3 carrots, cut in 1-inch pieces

1 pound baby Dutch potatoes

¼ pound mushrooms, halved

1 pound frozen pearl onions

1 ½ teaspoons red wine vinegar (to be added at the end)

Directions:

1. Pat the meat dry then season with flour, salt, and pepper. Sear in a skillet over medium heat. The meat should be evenly browned.
2. Place the meat in slow cooker and top with the bundle of thyme.
3. Turn off the heat under the skillet. Pour in the cognac deglaze the pan. Add wine and beef stock and continue stirring, putting the heat back on if necessary. Add tomato paste and stir until well-dissolved in the liquid.
4. Add the garlic, onion, carrots, potatoes, mushrooms, and onions to the slow cooker, and stir in liquid from skillet.
5. Cover and cook for 6-8 hours on LOW.
6. Remove the thyme stems and add the vinegar. Adjust seasoning, if needed.

NOTE: This soup contains alcohol and is not suitable for children.

Nutrition (per serving):

Calories 177

Fat 7 g

Carbs 6 g

Protein 16 g

Sodium 541 mg

Beef Stew

Serves: 8

Preparation time: 15 minutes

Cooking time: 8 hours on LOW

Ingredients:

For browning

2 pounds boneless chuck roast, trimmed, cut into 2-inch cubes

½ teaspoon salt

¼ teaspoon ground black pepper, divided

2 tablespoons olive oil

Beer mixture

1 tablespoon olive oil

2 large medium onions, diced

6 cloves garlic, sliced thinly

1 teaspoon salt

¼ teaspoon black pepper

12 ounces beer

1 cup beef stock, unsalted

Other ingredients

1 ½ pounds baby Dutch potatoes, halved

1 pound carrots, peeled, cut into 2-inch slices

4 sprigs of thyme

2 bay leaves

Slurry

¼ cup beef stock, unsalted

2 tablespoons all-purpose flour

1 tablespoon Dijon mustard

1 tablespoon red wine vinegar

Garnish

¼ cup parsley, chopped

Directions:

1. Heat the olive oil in a large skillet over medium heat. Sear and brown the seasoned meat evenly. Sprinkle with salt and pepper and transfer to the slow cooker.
2. In the same skillet, sauté garlic and onions in olive oil. Add the beer and boil for 2 minutes.
3. Add broth, salt, and pepper, and bring to a simmer. Transfer this mixture to the slow cooker, including oil and bits of meat stuck to the skillet, to add flavor to the stew.
4. Add the potatoes, carrots, thyme, and bay leaf.
5. Cover and cook for 7 hours on LOW.
6. Add the end of cooking time, the beef should be tender. Cooking time may be lengthened if needed.

7. Whisk the beef stock, flour, mustard and red wine vinegar together to make a slurry. Pour into the slow cooker and stir. Cook another 15 minutes or until thickened.
8. Remove thyme sprigs and bay leaves.
9. Serve garnished with parsley.

Nutrition (per serving)

Calories 386

Fat 18 g

Carbs 28 g

Protein 25 g

Sodium 509 mg

Chicken or Poultry Recipes

Chunky Brunswick Soup

Serves: 9

Preparation time: 10 minutes

Cooking time: 8 hours on HIGH

Ingredients:

2 cups frozen Southern-style hash brown potatoes, thawed

2 medium onions, chopped

2 cups low sodium chicken broth

1 ½ cups frozen lima beans, thawed

1 ¼ cups green bell pepper, diced

1 cup frozen cut okra, thawed

1 cup barbecue sauce

1 cup cooked chicken breast, cubed

½ cup celery, diced

½ teaspoon black pepper, freshly ground

¼ teaspoon salt

¾ pound pulled smoked pork, chopped

2 8-ounce cans unsalted tomato sauce

1 15-ounce can whole-kernel corn with sweet peppers, drained

1 14.5-ounce can unsalted diced tomatoes, undrained

Directions:

1. Put all the ingredients in a 7-quart slow cooker, then cover and cook for 8 hours on HIGH.

Nutrition (per serving):

Calories 316

Fat 8 g

Carbs 41 g

Protein 20 g

Sodium 649 mg

Classic Chicken Alphabet Soup

Serves: 6

Preparation time: 5 minutes

Cooking time: 7-8 hours on LOW, 4-5 hours on HIGH

Ingredients:

2 pounds boneless, skinless chicken thighs

4 carrots, cut into 1-inch pieces

4 stalks celery, cut into ½-inch pieces

1 medium onion, halved

2 garlic cloves, smashed

2 bay leaves

Salt and pepper

½ cup alphabet pasta (to be added towards the end)

¼ cup fresh flat-leaf parsley, chopped (to be added when soup is cooked)

Soda crackers, for serving

Directions:

1. Place the chicken, carrots, celery, onion, garlic, and bay leaves in the slow cooker. Season with salt and pepper.

2. Cover and cook for 4-5 hours on HIGH or 7-8 hours on LOW.

3. Twenty minutes before the cooking time is complete, remove the chicken to a dish.

4. Add the pasta to the slow cooker and stir. Continue cooking on HIGH for 15 to 20 minutes or until pasta is tender.
5. Shred the chicken while the pasta is cooking.
6. When the pasta is cooked, return the chicken to the soup. Sprinkle with parsley and stir.
7. Serve with crackers.

Nutrition (per serving):

Calories 293

Fat 12 g

Carbs 16 g

Protein 30 g

Sodium 464 mg

Cozy Chicken and Corn Chowder

Serves: 8

Preparation time: 15 minutes

Cooking time: 7-8 hours on LOW or 3-4 hours on HIGH

Ingredients:

1 pound boneless skinless chicken thighs, cut into 1-inch pieces

2 large red potatoes, diced

1 onion, diced

3 carrots, peeled and diced

2 stalks celery, diced

2 cups corn kernels

2 cups chicken broth

2 cups milk

3 cloves garlic, minced

½ teaspoon dried thyme

½ teaspoon dried oregano

Pinch of cayenne pepper

1 bay leaf

Salt and pepper

½ cup half and half

2 tablespoons cornstarch

2 tablespoons unsalted butter

5 slices bacon, cooked and diced

2 tablespoons chopped fresh chives

41

Directions:

1. Arrange the chicken, potatoes, onion, carrots, celery, corn, chicken broth, milk, garlic, and bay leaf in the slow cooker. Season with thyme, oregano, and cayenne pepper.
2. Cover and cook for 7-8 hours on LOW or for 3-4 hours on HIGH.
3. Whisk the cornstarch and half and half together in a bowl.
4. Thirty minutes before cooking is complete, stir in the half and half mixture. Add butter.
5. Cook 10 to 15 minutes more or until the soup is thick and creamy.
6. Serve garnished with bacon and chives.

Nutrition (per serving):

Calories 293

Fat 13 g

Carbs 26 g

Protein 19 g

Sodium 125 mg

Shanghai Imperial Duck Soup

Serves: 2

Preparation time: 20 minutes

Cooking time: 8 hours on LOW

Ingredients:

1 cooked Peking Duck, whole

4 cups water (more may be needed)

4-6 leaves of choy sum or Shanghai cabbage

4 shiitake mushrooms

2 7-ounce packets udon noodles

Sesame oil

White pepper

Thai basil leaves

Directions:

1. Rehydrate the shiitake mushrooms by soaking in hot water for 10 minutes. Set aside.
2. Soak udon noodles in hot, freshly-boiled water for 1 minute. Drain and place in a serving bowl. Set aside.
3. Place the duck in the slow cooker. Fill with enough water to cover.
4. Cover and cook for 8 hours on LOW or until the duck meat easily falls off the bone.

5. Remove the duck, transfer to a dish for shredding, and drop the choy sum into the hot duck broth in the slow cooker. Separate the breast part of the duck and slice thinly for garnishing. Shred the remaining meat.
6. Adjust the flavor of soup with salt and pepper, if needed.
7. Drain the shiitake mushrooms, and add to the prepared noodles, together with the shredded duck meat.
8. Pour broth over the noodle mixture.
9. Top with sliced duck breast and Thai basil leaves.
10. Add a few drops of sesame oil and sprinkle with white pepper before serving.

Nutrition (per serving):

Calories 363

Fat 10 g

Carbs 3 g

Protein 10 g

Sodium 623 mg

Chicken Soup with Wild Rice

Serves: 8

Preparation time: 10 minutes

Cooking time: 6-7 hours on LOW or 3-4 hours on HIGH

Ingredients:

2 pounds boneless skinless chicken breast

1 medium onion, chopped

3 carrots, peeled and chopped

3 stalks celery, chopped

2 cloves garlic, finely chopped

1 cup uncooked wild rice, rinsed and drained

2 bay leaves

½ teaspoon dried thyme

10 cups low-sodium chicken broth

¼ cup chopped fresh parsley

 Salt and pepper

Directions:

1. Arrange the chicken in the slow cooker, and add the onion, carrots, celery, garlic, rice, and bay leaves. Season with thyme, and pour in the broth.

2. Cover and cook for 6-7 hours on LOW or 3-4 hours on HIGH.

3. When cooked, remove the chicken and shred.

4. Return the shredded meat to slow cooker and stir. Season with salt and pepper.
5. Remove the bay leaves.
6. Garnish with parsley and serve.

Nutrition (per serving):

Calories 150

Fat 6 g

Carbs 18 g

Protein 7 g

Sodium 470 mg

Salsa and Chili Chicken Stew

Serves: 6

Preparation time: 15 minutes

Cooking time: 4-5 hours on HIGH

Ingredients:

1 pound boneless skinless chicken breasts

4 boneless skinless chicken thighs

2 potatoes, peeled and cut into 1 ½-inch pieces

1 10-ounce package frozen whole kernel corn

2 celery stalks, chopped

2 carrots, peeled and cut into chunks

1 onion, cut into ½-inch thick slices

2 cloves garlic, minced

1 cup bottled salsa

1 ½ teaspoons ground cumin

1 teaspoon chili powder

½ teaspoon freshly ground black pepper

2 ½ cups chicken broth, fat-free, reduced sodium

4 6-inch fresh corn tortillas, cut into strips

Chopped fresh parsley (optional)

Directions:

1. Combine all the ingredients in slow cooker.
2. Cover and cook for 4 hours on HIGH.
3. Remove the chicken and shred.

4. Return the shredded chicken to the slow cooker and stir in the tortilla strips.

5. Serve garnished with parsley.

Nutrition (per serving):

Calories 403

Fat 5 g

Carbs 55 g

Protein 35 g

Sodium 643 mg

Creamy Chicken Mushroom Soup

Serves: 4

Preparation time: 15 minutes

Cooking time: 8-9 hours on HIGH

Ingredients:

8 boneless skinless chicken thighs

8 ounces cremini mushrooms, stems trimmed, halved

4 carrots, cut into 1-inch pieces

2 sprigs fresh thyme

1 bay leaf

1 medium onion, chopped

1/3 cup all-purpose flour

½ cup water

Salt and black pepper

1 cup frozen peas

1 cup frozen green beans

1/3 cup heavy cream

Pre-baked puff pastry to cover soup bowls (optional)

Directions:

1. Place the mushrooms, carrots, onion, thyme, and bay leaf in the slow cooker. Mix the flour and water together, and pour over the vegetables. Mix.

2. Arrange the chicken on top. Season with salt and pepper.

3. Cover and cook for 7-8 hours on LOW or for 4-5 hours on HIGH. The chicken and vegetables should be tender.

4. Stir in the peas, green beans, and cream. Add more salt or pepper, if desired.

5. Cover and cook for 5-10 more minutes.

6. After ladling into bowls, cover with pre-baked puff pastry (optional).

Nutrition (per serving):

Calories 690

Fat 37 g

Carbs 47 g

Protein 41 g

Sodium 1,209 mg

Thai Chicken Soup with Curry and Coconut Milk

Serves: 6

Preparation time: 15 minutes

Cooking time: 4 hours on HIGH

Ingredients:

2 tablespoons red curry paste

2 12-ounce cans coconut milk

2 cups chicken stock

2 tablespoons fish sauce

2 tablespoons brown sugar

2 tablespoons peanut butter

1 ½ pounds chicken breast, cut into 1 ½-inch pieces

1 red bell pepper, seeded and sliced into ¼-inch slices

1 onion, thinly sliced

1 thumb of fresh ginger, minced

1 cup frozen peas, thawed

1 tablespoon lime juice

Cilantro for garnish

Cooked white rice

Directions:

1. Put the curry paste, coconut milk, chicken stock, fish sauce, brown sugar, and peanut butter into the slow cooker. Mix well.
2. Arrange the chicken on top and add bell pepper, onion, and ginger.
3. Cover and cook for 4 hours on HIGH.
4. Add the peas. Cook 30 minutes longer.
5. Stir in the lime juice.
6. Serve with cilantro and rice.

Nutrition (per serving):

Calories 147

Fat 5 g

Carbs 8 g

Protein 16 g

Sodium 977 mg

Soup with Turkey and Noodles

Serves: 8

Preparation time: 20 minutes

Cooking time: 9-10 hours on LOW

Ingredients:

7 cups turkey or chicken stock, or broth

3 cups leftover cooked turkey, shredded

1 large carrot, sliced

2 stalks celery, sliced

1 large white onion, diced

2 bay leaves

½ teaspoon thyme

8 ounces fettuccine noodles (broken up)

Salt and pepper

Directions:

1. Put the stock or broth, shredded turkey, carrot, celery, onion, bay leaves, and thyme into a slow cooker.
2. Cover and cook for 8 hours on LOW.
3. After the 8 hours of cooking, boil a pot of water on the stove. Add the noodles and cook for 12 minutes. Remove and drain.
4. Add drained noodles to the slow cooker. Cook for another 1 ½ hours on HIGH.

5. Noodles will be tender and soup will be thicker.

Nutrition (per serving):

Calories 204

Fat 5 g

Carbs 22 g

Protein 16 g

Sodium 610 mg

Chicken Pho (Traditional Vietnamese Chicken Noodle Soup)

Serves: 4

Preparation time: 25 minutes

Cooking time: 8-10 hours on LOW or 4-6 hours on HIGH

Ingredients:

½ pound chicken wing tips

1 ½ pounds mixed chicken pieces

½ medium-sized onion

3 thumbs ginger, sliced

2 tablespoons whole coriander seeds

4 pieces whole cloves

2 pieces whole star anise

2 tablespoons sugar

2 tablespoons fish sauce

1 bunch of cilantro stems, tied

Water

½ pound chicken breast, deboned and very finely sliced (to be cooked separately)

1 pound dried rice noodles (¼-inch thick)

12 cups bean sprouts, washed

½ cup red onions, finely sliced

½ lime, cut into 4 wedges

Cilantro leaves

Sriracha hot sauce (optional)

Hoisin sauce (optional).

Directions:

<u>For the broth</u>

1. Place the wing tips, chicken pieces, onion, ginger, coriander, cloves, star anise, sugar, fish sauce, and cilantro in the slow cooker.
2. Add water until slow cooker is about ¾ full.
3. Cover and cook for 8-10 hours on LOW or for 4-6 hours on HIGH.
4. Remove chicken (to be added later to noodles) and discard cilantro stems.
5. Strain the broth through cheesecloth. Discard the strained solids. All you want is the tasty, clear broth.
6. Adjust the taste of the broth with fish sauce and sugar, if needed.

<u>For the noodles and chicken breast topping</u>

7. In a large pot, boil enough water for the noodles.
8. In the meantime, soak the rice noodles in cool water for 5 minutes, then drain.
9. When the water starts to boil, lower heat and add finely sliced chicken breast for 1 to 5 minutes. Remove the chicken.
10. Next, add the drained rice noodles to the simmering water. Cook for 1 minute.

11. Remove the noodles and place in a large serving bowl, or divide among 4 small bowls.

Assembling the soup

12. Top the noodles with sliced chicken, bean sprouts, cilantro leaves, and red onion.
13. Finally, pour the broth over the noodles and toppings.
14. Serve with lime and condiments.

Nutrition (per serving):

Calories 390

Fat 6 g

Carbs 58 g

Protein 25 g

Sodium 1,200 mg

Pork Recipes

Split Pea Soup with Ham

Serves: 8

Preparation time: 15 minutes

Cooking time: 8 hours on LOW

Ingredients:

2 pounds smoked ham hocks

2 ¼ cups dried green split peas, rinsed and drained

1 ½ cups potatoes, cubed, peeled

5 garlic cloves, chopped

1 large onion, chopped

2 stalks celery, chopped

2 medium carrots, peeled and chopped

1 large bay leaf

Salt and pepper, to taste

6 cups water

½ cup light sour cream

Directions:

1. Place the split peas, potatoes, garlic, onion, celery, carrots, bay leaf, and ham hocks in the slow cooker, layering them as listed.
2. Cover and cook for 8 hours on LOW.

3. Remove the ham and shred or cut into bite-size pieces. Discard any bones.
4. Remove the bay leaf.
5. You may adjust the soup's texture and consistency by mashing the solids or by adding a little hot water to thin.
6. Stir in the cut or shredded ham.
7. Serve topped with sour cream.

Nutrition (per serving):

Calories 304

Fat 5 g

Carbs 45 g

Protein 22 g

Sodium 594 mg

Ham and White Bean Soup

Serves: 8

Preparation time: 15 minutes

Cooking time: 8-9 hours on LOW

Ingredients:

2 tablespoons olive oil

1 large onion, chopped

2 celery stalks, diced

2 medium carrots, diced

1 tablespoon fresh thyme, chopped

6 cloves garlic, chopped

2 pounds smoked ham hocks

1 cup dried Great Northern beans

2 26-ounce cartons chicken stock, unsalted

¼ cup fresh chives, minced

Black pepper, freshly ground

Directions:

1. Heat the olive oil in a skillet, and sauté the onion, celery, carrots, thyme and garlic over medium heat. Cook until the vegetables are tender. Transfer to a slow cooker, making sure to scrape any bits stuck to the pan as well.
2. Add the ham hocks, beans, and chicken stock.

3. Cover and cook for at least 8 hours on LOW. Beans should be of desired tenderness.

4. Remove the ham and cut into bite-sized pieces, discarding bones and excess fat.

5. Put the ham pieces back into the slow cooker and stir.

6. Cook 10 minutes longer for flavors to meld.

7. Serve sprinkled with chives and black pepper.

Nutrition (per serving):

Calories 260

Fat 5 g

Carbs 36 g

Protein 19 g

Sodium 639 mg

Bacon and Potato Soup

Serves: 8

Preparation time: 15 minutes

Cooking time: 8-9 hours on LOW

Ingredients:

½ cup bacon, pre-cooked crisp, crumbled (about 8 strips)

2 teaspoons bacon drippings

1 large onion, chopped

3 pounds potatoes, peeled, cut into ¼-inch slices

Non-stick cooking spray

½ cup water

2 4 ½-ounce cans chicken broth, fat-free, lower-sodium

½ teaspoon salt

½ teaspoon freshly ground black pepper

2 cups low-fat milk

¾ cup cheddar cheese, shredded

½ cup light sour cream

4 teaspoons fresh chives, chopped

Directions:

1. Heat the bacon drippings in a skillet over medium heat, and stir-fry the onions until tender.
2. Coat a slow cooker with non-stick spray.

3. Place the potato slices in slow cooker. Scrape in the sautéed onion and drippings as well.
4. Stir in the water, broth, salt, and pepper.
5. Cover and cook for 8 hours on LOW or until the potatoes are tender.
6. Mash potatoes. Stir in milk and cheese.
7. Set slow cooker to HIGH and cook about 20 minutes longer or until heated through.
8. Serve with sour cream, sprinkled with bacon and chives. Sprinkle more cheese, if desired.

Nutrition (per serving):

Calories 259

Fat 6 g

Carbs 38 g

Protein 13 g

Sodium 683 mg

Savory and Spicy Mexican Posole

Serves: 8

Preparation time: 10 minutes

Cooking time: 8 hours on LOW

Ingredients:

1 tablespoon canola oil

2 pounds pork tenderloin, cut into 1 ½-inch pieces

4 cups chicken broth, reduced sodium, fat-free

1 medium onion, chopped

1 ½ teaspoons ground cumin

1 teaspoon dried oregano

½ teaspoon black pepper, freshly ground

¼ teaspoon ground cloves

⅛ teaspoon red pepper, crushed

4 cloves garlic, minced

2 15 ½-ounce cans white hominy, rinsed, drained

2 4 ½-ounce cans chopped green chilies, undrained

1 cup packaged angel hair slaw

4 radishes, thinly sliced

1 small avocado, diced

Lime wedges (optional)

Directions:

1. Pat the pork with paper towels to dry.

2. Coat a skillet with the oil and brown the pork on all sides.

3. Place the pork, broth, onion, cumin, oregano, black pepper, cloves, garlic, hominy, and green chilies into the slow cooker.

4. Cover and cook for 8 hours on LOW.

5. Ladle into bowls, and top with slaw, radish, and avocado.

6. Serve with lime wedges.

Nutrition (per serving):

Calories 213

Fat 6 g

Carbs 12 g

Protein 27 g

Sodium 553 mg

Meat-Lover's Cassoulet

Serves: 8

Preparation time: 15 minutes

Cooking time: 5 hours on LOW

Ingredients:

2 strips bacon, preferably center-cut

2 cups onion, chopped

1 teaspoon dried thyme

½ teaspoon dried rosemary

3 cloves garlic, minced

2 14 ½-ounce cans diced tomatoes, drained

Salt and pepper

2 15-ounce cans Great Northern beans, rinsed and drained (divided)

1 pound boneless lean pork loin roast, trimmed and cut into 1-inch pieces

½ pound reduced-fat smoked sausage, cut into ½-inch pieces

Parmesan cheese, finely shredded

Flat-leaf parsley, chopped

Directions:

1. Heat a skillet over medium heat and cook bacon strips until crisp. Remove and crumble.

2. Using the drippings, brown the pork and sausage, remove from the pan, and set them aside. Add the onion, thyme, rosemary, and garlic to the pan, and cook for about 3 minutes.

3. Return the bacon to the skillet and add the tomatoes. Season with salt and pepper. Bring mixture to a boil.

4. Drain and rinse the beans. In a bowl, mash one can until the texture is coarse. Stir both cans into the pork mixture.

5. In the slow cooker, layer half of the bean mixture topped with half of the tomato mixture. Repeat layers.

6. Cover and cook for 5 hours on LOW.

7. If desired, after turning off heat, allow to stand 30 minutes to thicken.

8. Serve sprinkled with Parmesan and parsley.

Nutrition (per serving):

Calories 249

Fat 8 g

Carbs 24 g

Protein 22 g

Sodium 627 mg

Bacon and Lentil Tomato Curry

Serves: 6

Preparation time: 10 minutes

Cooking time: 8 hours on LOW

Ingredients:

6 strips bacon, preferably center-cut

1 large onion, chopped

4 cloves garlic, finely chopped

3 cups chicken broth, reduced sodium, fat free

1 cup dried lentils

1 medium carrot, chopped

2 celery stalks, chopped

2 teaspoons curry powder

½ teaspoon ground ginger

¼ teaspoon ground cinnamon

2 14 ½-ounce cans no-salt-added stewed tomatoes, undrained

½ cup half and half

2 tablespoons dry sherry

Directions:

1. Heat a skillet over medium heat and cook the bacon strips until crisp. Remove and crumble.
2. Using the drippings, sauté the onion and garlic for about 3 minutes. Scrape into slow cooker.

3. Place the chicken broth, lentils, carrot, celery, curry powder, ginger, cinnamon and tomatoes in the slow cooker.

4. Cover and cook for 8 hours on LOW.

5. Stir in the sherry and half and half.

6. Serve topped with bacon.

Nutrition (per serving):

Calories 218

Fat 4 g

Carbs 33 g

Protein 13 g

Sodium 445 mg

Pork and Black Bean Soup with Beer

Serves: 6

Preparation time: 15 minutes

Cooking time: 4-6 hours on HIGH

Ingredients:

2 12-ounce bottles of beer

3 cups water

1 tablespoon chopped canned chipotle chilies in adobo sauce, drained, sauce reserved

1 tablespoon adobo sauce

1 teaspoon ground cumin

1 large onion, chopped

2 cups dried black beans, rinsed

1 ½ pounds boneless pork shoulder

1 ½ teaspoons salt

½ cup sour cream

½ cup salsa

¼ cup fresh cilantro

Directions:

1. Put the beer, water, chilies, adobo sauce, cumin, onion, beans, pork, and salt into slow cooker.

2. Cover and cook for 4 to 6 hours on HIGH. You should be able to easily pull the pork apart into chunks.

3. Serve topped with sour cream, salsa, and cilantro.

Nutrition (per serving):

Calories 609

Fat 25 g

Carbs 55 g

Protein 36 g

Sodium 599 mg

Cajun Sausage and White Bean Soup

Serves: 6

Preparation time: 10 minutes

Cooking time: 7-8 hours on LOW or 4-5 hours on HIGH

Ingredients:

1 pound dried Great Northern beans

½ pound Cajun andouille sausage, sliced

1 large onion, chopped

2 stalks celery, chopped

4 sprigs fresh thyme

8 cups chicken broth, low-sodium

8 cups collard greens, leaves only, cut to 1-inch pieces

1 tablespoon red wine vinegar

Salt and pepper

Directions:

1. Set aside the last 3 ingredients.
2. Place the beans, sausage, onion, celery, thyme, and chicken broth in the slow cooker and stir.
3. Cover and cook for 7 to 8 hours on LOW or for 4 to 5 hours on HIGH. Beans should be tender.
4. Remove the thyme stems and drop in the collard greens. Cover and cook 15 minutes longer or until the greens are tender.
5. Add the vinegar, and salt and pepper to taste.

Nutrition (per serving):

Calories 393

Fat 8 g

Carbs 51 g

Protein 30 g

Sodium 670 mg

Mom's Tomato and Pork Soup

Serves: 8

Preparation time: 10 minutes

Cooking time: 4 hours 20 minutes on HIGH

Ingredients:

2 tablespoons olive oil

2 pounds boneless pork ribs, cut into bite-sized pieces

Salt and pepper to taste

1 tablespoon garlic, chopped

1 small onion, chopped

½ cup dry white wine

1 cup chicken stock

4 tomatoes, chopped

1 cup water

2 tablespoons fresh oregano, chopped

2 cups cauliflower florets, grated

Directions:

1. Pat the pork with paper towels to dry. Season with salt and pepper.
2. Coat a skillet with oil, and sear the meat until evenly browned.
3. Add the garlic and onion to the pan, and continue cooking for 2 minutes.

4. Add the chicken stock, wine, tomatoes, and water. Bring to a boil.
5. Transfer and scrape the contents of the skillet into the slow cooker. Cover and cook for 4 hours on HIGH. Meat should be tender and easy to pull apart with a fork.
6. Add the oregano and cauliflower. Cover and cook 20 minutes longer.

Nutrition (per serving):

Calories 326

Fat 22 g

Carbs 3 g

Protein 21 g

Sodium 945 mg

Pork Ramen

Serves: 8

Preparation time: minutes

Cooking time: 9 hours on LOW

Ingredients:

3 pounds boneless pork shoulder, cut into 3 equal pieces

Salt

1 onion, coarsely chopped

6 cloves garlic, chopped

2 thumbs of ginger, peeled and chopped

8 cups chicken broth, low-sodium (divided)

1 leek, chopped

4 ounces cremini mushrooms, brushed clean, coarsely chopped

Soy sauce, for seasoning

Sesame oil, for seasoning

1 ½ pounds, ramen noodles, cooked

4 eggs, soft-boiled, halved

4 green onions, finely chopped

Directions:

Optional browning step

1. Pat the meat with paper towels to dry. Season with salt.
2. Heat 2 tablespoons of vegetable oil a skillet and brown the pork over medium heat. When the meat has browned evenly, transfer to a slow cooker.
3. Drain any oil in excess of 2 tablespoons from the skillet. Use this to sauté onions.
4. Pour in 1 cup broth to deglaze the skillet. Stir in garlic and ginger, and loosen any brown bits from the skillet. Simmer for about 1 minute.
5. Pour deglazing broth over the pork in the slow cooker. Add the garlic, ginger, chicken broth, leek, and mushrooms.
6. Cover and cook for 8 hours on LOW. The pork is done when easy to pull apart with a fork.

If you skipped browning step

1. Simply put the pork, onion, garlic, ginger, broth, leek, and mushrooms into the slow cooker.
2. Cover and cook for 8 hours on LOW. Pork is done when easy to pull apart with a fork.

Assembling the ramen

1. Remove the pork and pull apart into chunks, removing any excess fat.
2. Strain the broth and discard solids. Skim off any fat on the surface of the broth.
3. Pour the broth back into the slow cooker, and add the pork chunks.
4. Season with soy sauce and sesame oil to adjust flavor of broth.
5. Cover again and cook 30 minutes more.
6. Divide noodles among 8 individual bowls.
7. Ladle pork and broth equally into bowls. Top each with green onion and half a soft-boiled egg.
8. Serve immediately.

Nutrition (per serving):

Calories 483

Fat 6 g

Carbs 74 g

Protein 28 g

Sodium 980 mg

Fish and Seafood Recipes

San Francisco Seafood Stew

Serves: 8

Preparation time: 20 minutes

Cooking time: 4 hours 30 minutes on HIGH

Ingredients:

1 28-ounce can diced tomatoes, undrained

2 medium onions, chopped

3 celery stalks, chopped

1 8-ounce bottle clam juice

1 6-ounce can tomato paste

½ cup white wine (or vegetable broth)

5 cloves garlic, minced

1 tablespoon red wine vinegar

1 tablespoon olive oil

2 teaspoons Italian seasoning

1 bay leaf

½ teaspoon sugar

1 pound haddock fillets, cut into 1-inch pieces

1 pound shrimp (41-50 pieces per pound), uncooked, peeled and deveined

1 6-ounce can chopped clams, undrained

1 6-ounce can lump crabmeat, drained

2 tablespoons minced fresh parsley

Directions:

1. Place the tomatoes, onions, celery, clam juice, tomato paste, wine or broth, garlic, vinegar, olive oil, Italian seasoning, bay leaf, and sugar in a slow cooker.
2. Cover and cook 4-5 hours on LOW.
3. Add the haddock, shrimp, clams, and crabmeat. Cover and cook 20-30 minutes longer. The soup is ready when the fish can easily be flaked and shrimp are pink in color.
4. Remove bay leaf.
5. Stir in parsley and serve.

Nutrition (per serving):

Calories 205

Fat 3 g

Carbs 15 g

Protein 29 g

Sodium 483 mg

Fisherman's Stew

Serves: 6

Preparation time: 35 minutes

Cooking time: 8 hours on LOW

Ingredients:

2 tablespoons olive oil

2 cloves garlic, finely chopped

1 cup baby carrots, sliced ¼-inch thick

6 large Roma tomatoes sliced, quartered

1 green bell pepper, chopped

½ teaspoon fennel seed

1 cup water

1 8-ounce bottle clam juice

1 pound cod, cut into 1-inch cubes

½ pound medium shrimp, uncooked, peeled and deveined

1 teaspoon sugar

1 teaspoon dried basil leaves

½ teaspoon salt

¼ teaspoon red pepper sauce

2 tablespoons fresh parsley, chopped

Directions:

1. Stir the olive oil, garlic, carrots, tomatoes, green pepper, fennel seed, water, and clam juice together in the slow cooker.
2. Cover and cook 8 to 9 hours on LOW. Vegetables should be tender.
3. Twenty minutes before serving, add cod, shrimp, sugar, basil, salt, and pepper sauce. Cover and cook 15 to 20 minutes on HIGH. The soup is ready when the fish can easily be flaked and shrimp are pink in color.

Nutrition (per serving):

Calories 180

Fat 6 g

Carbs 5 g

Protein 22 g

Sodium 332 mg

Fish Chowder

Serves: 6-8

Preparation time: 15 minutes

Cooking time: 4 hours on LOW

Ingredients:

4 slices bacon, chopped

2 teaspoons bacon drippings

1 onion, chopped

2 cloves garlic, minced

6 cups chicken stock

1 cup whole corn kernels

2 large potatoes, diced

3 stalks celery, diced

2 large carrots, diced

Ground black pepper to taste

Red pepper flakes to taste

1 cup scallops

1 cup uncooked medium shrimp, peeled and deveined

¼ pound halibut, cut into bite-size pieces

1 12-ounce can evaporated milk

Directions:

1. Brown the bacon in a skillet over medium heat. Drain off any drippings in excess of about 2 teaspoons.
2. Sauté onion and garlic along with bacon until vegetables are tender.
3. Scrape contents of skillet into slow cooker.
4. Stir in the chicken stock, corn kernels, potatoes, celery, carrots, black pepper, and red pepper flakes.
5. Cover and cook for 3 hours on HIGH. The vegetables should be tender.
6. Add scallops, shrimp, and halibut. Cover and continue cooking for about 30 minutes to 1 hour more. The soup is ready when fish can easily be flaked and shrimp are pink in color.
7. Pour in evaporated milk and stir until heated through.

Nutrition (per serving):

Calories 190

Fat 5 g

Carbs 12 g

Protein 24 g

Sodium 586 mg

Seafood Gumbo

Serves: 6-8

Preparation time: 20 minutes

Cooking time: 5 hours on LOW, 2 hours 30 minutes on HIGH

Ingredients:

8-10 bacon strips, sliced

2 stalks celery, sliced

1 medium onion, sliced

1 green pepper, chopped

2 garlic cloves, minced

2 cups chicken broth

1 14-ounce can diced tomatoes, undrained

2 tablespoons Worcestershire sauce

2 teaspoons salt

1 teaspoon dried thyme leaves

1 pound large raw shrimp, peeled, deveined

1 pound fresh or frozen crabmeat

1 10-ounce box frozen okra, thawed and sliced into ½-inch pieces

Directions:

1. Brown the bacon in a skillet over medium heat. When crisp, drain and transfer to a slow cooker.

2. Drain off drippings, leaving just enough to coat the skillet. Sauté celery, onion, green pepper, and garlic until vegetables are tender.

3. Transfer the sautéed vegetables to the slow cooker. Add the broth, tomatoes, Worcestershire sauce, salt, and thyme.

4. Cover and cook for 4 hours on LOW, or for 2 hours on HIGH.

5. Add the shrimp, crabmeat, and okra. Cover and cook 1 hour longer on LOW or 30 minutes longer on HIGH.

Nutrition (per serving):

Calories 273

Fat 8 g

Carbs 11 g

Protein 4 g

Sodium 1757 mg

Seafood Chowder

Serves: 6-8

Preparation time: 25 minutes

Cooking time: 8-9 hours on HIGH

Ingredients:

Half bulb fennel, cored and diced

2 potatoes, peeled and diced

1 onion, diced

1 celery stalk, diced

2 bay leaves

1 tablespoon dried thyme

1 teaspoon salt

¼ teaspoon pepper

¼ teaspoon cayenne powder

1 8-ounce bottle clam juice

2 cups water

1 cup cream

3 tablespoons cornstarch

1 ½ pound skinless salmon fillets, cut in 1-inch pieces

½ pound large shrimp, peeled and deveined

5 sea scallops, halved horizontally

¼ cup chopped fresh parsley

Directions:

1. Place the fennel, potatoes, onion, celery, bay leaves, thyme, salt, pepper, cayenne powder and water in the slow cooker and stir.
2. Cover and cook for 8 hours on LOW. The potatoes should be tender.
3. Remove the bay leaves.
4. In a bowl, whisk the cream with cornstarch until smooth. Stir into the slow cooker together with seafood.
5. Cover and cook for about 30 minutes on HIGH or until the fish flakes easily and the soup has thickened.
6. Stir in parsley and serve.

Nutrition (per serving):

Calories 378

Fat 23 g

Carbs 16 g

Protein 27 g

Sodium 493 mg

White Bean Soup with Shrimp

Serves: 8

Preparation time: 15 minutes

Cooking time: 6-8 hours on LOW

Ingredients:

2 strips thick-cut bacon, unflavored

1 large onion, diced

2 cloves garlic, minced

1 pound kale, washed and roughly chopped

1 cup dried barley

1 ½ cups dried navy beans

6 cups low sodium chicken broth

4 cups water

8 ounces cooked shrimp

Directions:

1. Brown the bacon in a skillet over medium heat. When crisp, drain and transfer to slow cooker.
2. Drain off the drippings, leaving just enough to coat the skillet. Sauté the onion and garlic until tender. Transfer to a slow cooker.
3. Place kale, barley, and beans in the slow cooker.
4. Pour in the broth and water, and stir.

5. Cover and cook for 6-8 hours on LOW. Check occasionally to see if more water needs to be added.

6. About 20 minutes before end of cooking, add the cooked shrimps and stir to heat through.

Nutrition (per serving):

Calories 149

Fat 3 g

Carbs 15g

Protein 16 g

Sodium 392 mg

Lobster Chowder

Serves: 10-12

Preparation time: 15 minutes

Cooking time: 10 hours on LOW or 5 hours on HIGH

Ingredients:

1 ½ pounds cooked lobster meat, cut into bite-sized pieces

3 ½ cups potatoes, peeled and cubed

1 ½ cups whole corn kernels

1 medium onion, chopped

½ teaspoon paprika

½ teaspoon cumin

1 teaspoon thyme

1 teaspoon salt

1 teaspoon basil

½ teaspoon white ground pepper

1 teaspoon dried minced garlic

¼ cup all-purpose flour

1 ½ cups lobster stock (or seafood stock)

1 jalapeno, diced

4 strips bacon, thick cut

2 teaspoons bacon drippings

3 ½ cups half and half

Directions:

1. Brown the bacon in a skillet. Drain and crumble. Set aside.
2. Spoon 2 teaspoons of drippings into a slow cooker.
3. Place the potatoes, corn. Onion, paprika, cumin, thyme, salt, basil, white pepper, garlic, and jalapeno in the slow cooker. Gradually mix the lobster stock into the flour until smooth, and stir in with other ingredients.
4. Cover and cook for 5 hours on HIGH or for 10 hours on LOW.
5. Thirty minutes before cooking time ends, add the lobster pieces and whisk in half and half. Cover and continue cooking.
6. Serve sprinkled with crumbled bacon.

Nutrition (per serving):

Calories 130

Fat 4 g

Carbs 21 g

Protein 5 g

Sodium 340 mg

Crab and Corn Soup

Serves: 6

Preparation time: 10 minutes

Cooking time: 8 hours on LOW or 4 hours on HIGH

Ingredients:

1 quart chicken stock

1 tablespoon butter

1 large onion, chopped

6 cups corn kernels (fresh or frozen)

2 cloves garlic, chopped

1 teaspoon salt

½ teaspoon cayenne pepper

1 6-ounce can lump crabmeat, drained

1 cup half and half or heavy cream

1 avocado, cubed, for garnish

Directions:

1. Place the chicken stock, butter, onion, corn kernels, garlic, salt, cayenne pepper, and crabmeat in the slow cooker.
2. Cover and cook for 4 hours on HIGH or for 8 hours on LOW.

3. Blend with an immersion blender to get a smooth, thick consistency. (A regular blender may also be used. Puree in small batches to prevent spillage. Be careful, liquid is hot! Remove lid insert to allow steam to escape.)
4. Stir in half and half.
5. Serve topped with avocado

Nutrition (per serving):

Calories 250

Fat 14 g

Carbs 25 g

Protein 5 g

Sodium 960 mg

Shrimp Bisque

Serves: 6

Preparation time: 10 minutes

Cooking time: 3 hours on HIGH

Ingredients:

3 tablespoons butter

2 medium leeks, chopped

3 cloves garlic, minced

⅓ cup tomato paste

1 14-ounce can petite diced tomatoes

¼ cup dry sherry

1½ cups corn kernels

2 teaspoons Old Bay seasoning (or use Creole seasoning)

2 teaspoons salt

1 teaspoon pepper

4 cups seafood stock

¼ cup all-purpose flour

1 pound shrimp, peeled and deveined, chopped

1 cup heavy cream

Directions:

1. Melt butter in a skillet over medium heat. Sauté the onions and leeks until tender. Add stock and

sherry to deglaze, bringing to a boil. Transfer to slow cooker, including any brown bits.

2. Place the garlic, tomato paste, tomatoes, sherry, corn, Old Bay or Creole seasoning, salt and pepper in the slow cooker.

3. Whisk a small amount of the seafood stock into the flour until smooth. Add to the slow cooker together with the rest of the fish stock, and mix well.

4. Cook in your slow cooker for 4 hours on LOW or for 2 hours on HIGH.

5. If desired, thirty minutes before cooking is complete, puree with an immersion blender for a smoother texture. (A regular blender may also be used. Puree in small batches to prevent spillage. Be careful, liquid is hot! Remove lid insert to allow steam to escape.)

6. Stir in the shrimp and cream.

7. Continue heating 30 minutes more or until shrimp is pink in color.

Nutrition (per serving):

Calories 302

Fat 19 g

Carbs 10 g

Protein 14 g

Sodium 1,683 mg

Vegetarian Recipes

Wisconsin Beer and Cheese Soup

Serves: 6

Preparation time: 10 minutes

Cooking time: 7 hours and 20 minutes on LOW

Ingredients:

4 cups vegetable broth (divided)

1 12-ounce bottle lager beer

2 medium carrots, finely diced

1 stalk celery, finely diced

1 large onion, finely diced

3 cloves garlic, minced

1 teaspoon salt

½ teaspoon white pepper

1 teaspoon Worcestershire sauce

1 teaspoon Dijon mustard

3 cups sharp cheddar cheese, shredded

½ cup heavy cream

¼ cup cornstarch

Directions:

1. Mix ½ cup of broth with the cornstarch until dissolved. Set aside.
2. Place the remaining broth, together with the beer, carrots, celery, onion, garlic, salt, pepper, Worcestershire sauce, and mustard into the slow cooker. Stir.
3. Cover and cook for 6-8 hours on LOW.
4. Whisk in the cream, continually whisking while gradually adding cheese. Whisk the slurry of broth and cornstarch until smooth and add to the soup.
5. Cover and cook 20 minutes longer.
6. Use an immersion blender until smooth, or transfer to blender. Puree in small batches to prevent spillage. Be careful, liquid is hot! Remove lid insert to allow steam to escape.
7. Traditionally served with pretzel bread.

Nutrition (per serving):

Calories 338

Fat 25 g

Carbs 10 g

Protein 16 g

Sodium 480 mg

Rich Butternut Squash Soup with Parsnips

Serves: 8

Preparation time: 10 minutes

Cooking time: 6 hours on LOW

Ingredients:

1 large sweet onion, chopped

3 large parsnips, peeled and chopped

1 large Granny Smith apple, peeled and chopped

¼ teaspoon salt

1 teaspoon freshly ground black pepper

3 cups water

2 cups chicken broth, reduced sodium, fat-free

3 12-ounce packages frozen butternut squash, thawed

2 tablespoons whipping cream

⅛ teaspoon paprika

⅛ teaspoon ground cumin

½ cup light sour cream

Chopped fresh chives (optional)

Directions:

1. Place the onion, parsnips, apple, salt, pepper, water, broth and squash in the slow cooker. Stir.
2. Cover and cook for 6 hours on LOW.

3. Puree using an immersion blender until smooth. (A regular blender may also be used. Puree in small batches to prevent spillage. Be careful, liquid is hot! Remove lid insert to allow steam to escape.)
4. Stir in the whipping cream, paprika, and cumin.
5. Serve with a dollop of sour cream on top, sprinkled with chives.

Nutrition (per serving):

Calories 132

Fat 5 g

Carbs 30 g

Protein 4 g

Sodium 228 mg

Minestrone Soup

Serves: 8

Preparation time: 10 minutes

Cooking time: 8 hours on LOW

Ingredients:

1 14 ½-ounce can diced tomatoes

2 cups carrots, peeled and chopped

2 cups potatoes, peeled and chopped

3 stalks celery, chopped

1 white onion, diced

4 cloves garlic, minced

1 tablespoon Italian seasoning

1 teaspoon salt

½ teaspoon pepper

2 bay leaves

4 cups vegetable stock, low sodium

2 cups water

3 cups tomato juice

1 15-ounce can red kidney beans, drained and rinsed

1 15-ounce can cannellini beans, drained and rinsed

1 ½ cups zucchini, diced

1 cups elbow macaroni

1 15-ounce can green beans, drained

Parmesan cheese, grated, for garnish (optional)

Directions:

1. Combine the tomatoes, carrots, potatoes, celery, onion, garlic, Italian seasoning, salt, pepper, stock, water, and tomato juice in the slow cooker.
2. Cover and cook for 6-8 hours on LOW or for 3-4 hours on HIGH.
3. Add the red kidney beans, cannellini beans, zucchini, green beans, and pasta.
4. Cook for an additional 10-15 minutes on HIGH or until pasta is tender.
5. Serve sprinkled with grated Parmesan cheese, if desired.

Nutrition (per serving):

Calories 170

Fat 5g

Carbs 26 g

Protein 5 g

Sodium 884 mg

Tasty Veggie Lasagna Soup

Serves: 8

Preparation time: 15 minutes

Cooking time: 7 hours on LOW

Ingredients:

For Soup

1 medium onion, chopped

3 cloves garlic, minced

1 28-ounce can crushed tomatoes

1 15-ounce can tomato sauce

4 cups vegetable broth, low sodium

1 15-ounce can cannellini beans or white kidney beans, drained

1 cup brown mushrooms, sliced

1 medium zucchini, sliced

2 teaspoons dried basil

1 ½ teaspoons dried oregano

½ teaspoon dried thyme

2 bay leaves

Salt and pepper, to taste

6 ounces lasagna pasta, broken into bite-sized pieces

4 cups baby spinach, chopped

For cheese topping

1 cup ricotta cheese

½ cup mozzarella cheese

¼ cup Parmesan cheese

Fresh parsley, chopped

Directions:

1. Combine the onion, garlic, tomatoes, vegetable broth, beans, mushrooms, zucchini, basil, oregano, thyme, bay leaves, salt, and pepper in the slow cooker. Stir.
2. Cover and cook for 7 hours on LOW.
3. Thirty minutes before cooking ends, add the pasta. Cover again and cook until pasta is tender. Add spinach and allow to wilt in hot soup.
4. In a bowl, mix the ricotta, mozzarella, Parmesan, and parsley. Ladle the soup into bowls and serve with the topping.

Nutrition (per serving):

Calories 188

Fat 9 g

Carbs 13 g

Protein 18 g

Sodium 628 mg

Bean and Squash Chili

Serves: 6

Preparation time: 15 minutes

Cooking time: 8 hours on LOW

Ingredients:

1 tablespoon olive oil

1 large onion, chopped

1 clove garlic, minced

3 red bell peppers, chopped

2 tablespoons chili powder

½ teaspoon ground cumin

2 12-ounce packages cubed butternut squash

3 cups cooked pinto beans

1 ½ cups water

1 cup frozen whole-kernel corn

1 teaspoon salt

1 14 ½-ounce can crushed tomatoes, undrained

1 14 ½-ounce can chopped green chilies, undrained

¾ cup queso fresco or feta, crumbled

Lime wedges

Directions:

1. Heat the oil in a skillet. Sauté the onion, garlic, and bell pepper. Season with chili and cumin while sautéing. Transfer to slow cooker.
2. Add the squash, pinto beans, water, corn, salt, tomatoes, and chilies. Cover and cook for 8 hours on LOW. Vegetables should be tender and soup should be thick.
3. Serve topped with cheese and lime.

Nutrition (per serving):

Calories 320

Fat 6 g

Carbs 56 g

Protein 15 g

Sodium 650 mg

Spicy Caribbean Soup

Serves: 8

Preparation time: 15 minutes

Cooking time: 8 hours on LOW

Ingredients:

1 tablespoon olive oil

1 large red onion, chopped

1 green bell pepper, diced

1 red bell pepper, diced

2 jalapeño peppers, finely chopped

1 whole garlic head, peeled and minced

¼ cup tomato paste, unsalted

4 cups vegetable broth, divided

1 teaspoon dried thyme

1 teaspoon ground cumin

½ teaspoon ground ginger

½ teaspoon ground allspice

¼ teaspoon ground red pepper

⅛ teaspoon salt

2 15-ounce cans no-salt-added black beans, rinsed and drained

½ cup coconut milk

½ cup fresh cilantro, chopped

8 lime wedges

Directions:

1. Heat the oil in a skillet over medium heat. Sauté the onion, red peppers, green peppers, and jalapeno until fragrant. Add the garlic and sauté a little longer. Add 1 cup of broth and tomato paste. Stir to deglaze pan. Transfer the broth mixture to a slow cooker.
2. Add the rest of the broth, thyme, cumin, ginger, allspice, ground red pepper, salt, and beans. Stir.
3. Cover and cook for 8 hours on LOW. Beans should be tender.
4. Whisk in the coconut milk.
5. Serve with lime wedges and topped with cilantro.

Nutrition (per serving):

Calories 143

Fat 5 g

Carbs 20 g

Protein 6 g

Sodium 333 mg

Serrano Pepper and Black Bean Soup

Serves: 6

Preparation time: 15 minutes

Cooking time: 10 hours on LOW

Ingredients:

2 cups dried black beans, cleaned, soaked overnight and drained

4 cups organic vegetable broth

2 onions, chopped

1 cup water

1 tablespoon ground cumin

3 bay leaves

1 serrano pepper, finely chopped

2 tablespoons fresh lime juice

1 teaspoon salt

¼ cup chopped fresh cilantro

3 tablespoons reduced-fat sour cream

Directions:

1. Combine the beans, broth, onions, water, cumin, bay leaves, and serrano pepper in the slow cooker.
2. Cover and cook for 10 hours on LOW.
3. Remove the bay leaves, season with salt, and stir in lime juice.

4. Serve topped with sour cream and cilantro.

Nutrition (per serving):

Calories 286

Fat 2 g

Carbs 51 g

Protein 17 g

Sodium 697 mg

Hot and Sour Soup

Serves: 6-8

Preparation time: 15 minutes

Cooking time: 8 hours on LOW

Ingredients:

1 10-ounce package mushrooms, sliced

8 fresh shiitake mushroom caps, sliced

1 8-ounce can bamboo shoots, drained and julienned

4 cloves garlic, minced

1 15-ounce package tofu, cubed

2 tablespoons grated fresh ginger (divided)

4 cups water

2 tablespoons vegan chicken-flavored bouillon

2 tablespoons soy sauce

1 teaspoon sesame oil

1 teaspoon chili paste

2 tablespoons rice wine vinegar

1 ½ cups peas, fresh or frozen

Directions:

1. Combine mushrooms, bamboo shoots, garlic, tofu, 1 tablespoon of ginger, water, bouillon, soy sauce, sesame oil, chili paste, and vinegar in the slow cooker. Cook for 6-8 hours on LOW. The mushrooms and bamboo shoots should be tender.
2. Add the peas and remaining 1 tablespoon ginger. Stir.
3. Adjust taste with vinegar or chili paste, if needed.
4. Serve with a few more drops sesame oil and the chili paste on the side.

Nutrition (per serving):

Calories 208

Fat 7 g

Carbs 22 g

Protein 19 g

Sodium 1088 mg

African-Style Peanut Soup

Serves: 8

Preparation time: 10 minutes

Cooking time: 6-8 hours on LOW or 4 hours on HIGH

Ingredients:

1 yellow onion, diced

2 spring onions, chopped

2 red bell peppers, chopped

4 cloves garlic, minced

1 28-ounce can crushed tomatoes, undrained

8 cups vegetable broth

¼ teaspoon black pepper

1 teaspoon ground cumin

¼ teaspoon chili powder

¼ cup uncooked brown lentils

½ cup uncooked brown rice

1 cup peanut butter

Sour cream and Tabasco sauce for topping

Directions:

1. Combine the onions, peppers, garlic, tomatoes, broth, black pepper, cumin, chili powder, lentils, and rice in the slow cooker.
2. Cover and cook for 6-8 hours on LOW or 4 hours on HIGH. The onions should be translucent.
3. Stir in the butter and cook 30 minutes more on HIGH.
4. Serve topped with sour cream and Tabasco sauce.

Nutrition (per serving):

Calories 245

Fat 7 g

Carbs 39 g

Protein 10 g

Sodium 819 mg

Tomato Soup with Basil

Serves: 6

Preparation time: 15 minutes

Cooking time: 6-7 hours on LOW or 5 hours on HIGH

Ingredients:

3 large carrots, peeled and chopped

2 celery stalks, diced

2 medium onions, chopped

4 whole cloves garlic, peeled

4 28-ounce cans whole peeled tomatoes

1 quart chicken broth, low sodium

½ cup fresh basil leaves, roughly chopped

Salt and pepper to taste

Cream and Parmesan cheese (optional)

Directions:

1. Combine the carrots, celery, onions, garlic, tomatoes, chicken broth, and basil in the slow cooker.
2. Cover and cook for 6-7 hours on LOW or for 5 hours on HIGH. The tomatoes should be soft and easy to puree.
3. Use an immersion blender to puree.

4. If using cream, blend it in now. Season to taste with salt and pepper.

5. Serve garnished with grated Parmesan and more basil leaves, if desired.

Nutrition (per serving):

Calories 130

Fat 1 g

Carbs 28 g

Protein 4 g

Sodium 470 mg

Sweet Potato Soup

Serves: 4

Preparation time: 10 minutes

Cooking time: 3 hours on HIGH

Ingredients:

2 sweet potatoes, peeled and diced

½ onion, minced

1 14-ounce can light coconut milk

1 cup vegetable broth

2 cloves garlic, minced

1 teaspoon dried basil

Salt and pepper

Directions:

1. Place all the ingredients in a slow cooker and stir.
2. Cover and cook for 3 hours on HIGH.
3. Puree with an immersion blender until the soup is smooth.

Nutrition (per serving):

Calories 127

Fat 5 g

Carbs 20 g

Protein 1 g

Sodium 159 mg

Conclusion

The slow cooker can be your friend and helper in all your cooking adventures. If you've read the recipes and think they sound mouth-watering, go ahead and try them out! Perhaps you've already tested some of the recipes and enjoyed the warmth and comfort that soup provides. My hope is that these recipes would become a family tradition to be enjoyed, cherished, and passed on to others.

About the Author

Louise Davidson is an avid cook who likes simple flavors and easy-to-make meals. She lives in Tennessee with her husband, her three grown children, her two dogs, and the family cat Whiskers. She loves the outdoor and has mastered the art of camp cooking on open fires and barbecue grills.

In colder months, she loves to whip up some slow cooker meals, and uses her favorite cooking tools in her kitchen, the cast iron pans, and Dutch oven. She also is very busy preparing Christmas treats for her extended family and friends. She gets busy baking for the holiday season sometimes as early as October. Her recipes are cherished by everyone who has tasted her foods and holiday treats.

Louise is a part-time writer of cookbooks, sharing her love of food, her experience, and her family's secret recipes with her readers.

She also loves to learn and share tips and tricks to make life.

More Books from Louise Davidson

Just click on any cover to check them out.

Cooking Conversion Charts

1. Volumes

US Fluid Oz.	US	US Dry Oz.	Metric Liquid ml
¼ oz.	2 tsp.	1 oz.	10 ml.
½ oz.	1 tbsp.	2 oz.	15 ml.
1 oz.	2 tbsp.	3 oz.	30 ml.
2 oz.	¼ cup	3½ oz.	60 ml.
4 oz.	½ cup	4 oz.	125 ml.
6 oz.	¾ cup	6 oz.	175 ml.
8 oz.	1 cup	8 oz.	250 ml.

Tsp.= teaspoon - tbsp.= tablespoon – oz.= ounce – ml.= millimeter

2. Oven Temperatures

Celsius (°C)	Fahrenheit (°F)
90	220
110	225
120	250
140	275
150	300
160	325
180	350
190	375
200	400
215	425
230	450
250	475
260	500

Made in the USA
Middletown, DE
15 October 2022

12831423R00076